What is a Trademark

Fifth Edition

AMERICAN**BAR**ASSOCIATION
Intellectual Property
Law Section

Printed in the United States of America.

28 27 26 25 24   5 4 3 2 1

ISBN: 978-1-63905-442-8
e-ISBN: 978-1-63905-443-5

Discounts are available for books ordered in bulk. Special consideration is given to state bars, CLE programs, and other bar-related organizations. Inquire at Book Publishing, ABA Publishing, American Bar Association, 321 N. Clark Street, Chicago, Illinois 60654-7598.

www.shopABA.org

Contents

What Is a Trademark?

Two hundred years ago, trademark protection was the poorer cousin to the patent and copyright protection systems. While protection of an inventor's discovery or an author's writing was the subject of a constitutional mandate, protection of trademarks was left to the common law (the part of United States law derived from custom and judicial precedent rather than statutes). There was reportedly little public interest in trademark protection.[1]

Today, trademarks may be protected under both state and federal statutes, as well as the common law. Many marks for consumer products and services such as electronic devices, social media platforms, and electronic marketplaces are worth hundreds of millions of dollars. Public interest in trademark protection is high, and trademarks are often among a business's most valuable assets.

The Nature of a Mark

What It Is

There are two primary types of marks—trademarks and service marks. The Trademark Act of 1946, also known as the Lanham Act, defines a trademark as any word, name, symbol, device, or any combination thereof used or intended to be used to identify and distinguish the goods of one seller or provider from those of others and to indicate the source of the goods.[2] The Lanham Act provides a similar definition for service marks, which are marks identifying services (e.g., banking, dry cleaning, or restaurant

---

1. Edmund W. Kitch & Harvey S. Perlman, Legal Regulation of the Competitive Process (3d ed. 1986); *see also* Frank I. Schechter, The Historical Foundations of the Law Relating to Trademarks (Columbia Univ. Press 1925).
2. 15 U.S.C. § 1127; Lanham Act § 45.

services) rather than goods. As used hereafter, the terms "trademark" and "mark" include service marks. Although not found in the statute, the term "brand name" is sometimes used synonymously with "trademark."

What It Does

A trademark has several functions. Arguably, the primary function is to identify and distinguish the source of the goods or services in connection with which the trademark is used.[3] It is unnecessary for the purchaser to know the identity of the source of goods as long as he or she recognizes that all goods bearing a particular mark originate from a common, albeit anonymous, source.[4] For example, while most people probably do not know that Big Heart Pet Brands makes 9 LIVES cat food, they most likely do believe that all cat food labeled 9 LIVES comes from a single source.

Trademarks also provide quality assurance. For example, a consumer dining at a MCDONALD'S or a RUTH'S CHRIS STEAK HOUSE restaurant expects the nature and quality of the food served will be the same as that served at other restaurants bearing that name. A trademark obliges its owner to maintain a consistent level of quality for the benefit of consumers, who need to rely on that consistent level of quality.

What It Is Not

Although the two are closely related, a trademark is not the same as a trade name. The term "trade name" applies to names used to identify a business or commercial establishment,[5] such as a legal corporate name or an assumed name ("doing business as" [dba]). Thus, while trademarks are associated with goods and services, trade names identify businesses.

---

3. *Id.*

4. *Id.* ("The term 'trademark' includes any word, name, symbol, or device, or any combination thereof . . . to indicate the source of the goods, even if that source is unknown.")

5. *Id.* ("The terms 'trade name' and 'commercial name' mean any name used by a person to identify his or her business or vocation.")

Possible Types of Marks

Provided it meets the three prerequisites for protection discussed below, virtually anything capable of indicating the source of goods or services may serve as a mark. A few examples are discussed below.

Letters and numbers may qualify as protectable marks. For example, ABC, CBS, and NBC are readily recognizable as the service marks of major radio and television broadcasting networks. Alphanumeric combinations such as V-8 vegetable juice and 7-ELEVEN convenience stores are also familiar marks.

Slogans can function as marks. For example, THE BREAKFAST OF CHAMPIONS indicates the source of WHEATIES breakfast cereal. Similarly, BOUNTY uses the slogan THE QUICKER PICKER UPPER as a trademark for its paper towels, and NIKE uses the slogan JUST DO IT for its sports apparel.

A color or combination of colors may function as an indicator of source and be registered as a mark[6] but only on a showing of secondary meaning or, in other words, recognition among consumers that the claimed mark *is* a mark. One example of a registered color mark is the red sole on high heels designed by Christian Louboutin.[7] Musical notes and other sounds have also been federally registered. The combination of notes "G, E, and C," used by the National Broadcasting Company, were originally registered by the *General Electric Company.*[8] Federal registrations have even been granted for a particular fragrance, reminiscent of plumeria, used to identify sewing thread,[9] as well as for motions[10] and textures.[11]

Finally, a mark can consist of such things as a product's shape, size, and packaging.[12] Likewise, even a business's overall image can potentially

---

6. *See* Qualitex Co. v. Jacobson Prods. Co., 514 U.S. 159 (1995).

7. U.S. Registration No. 3,361,597.

8. *In re* Gen. Elec. Broad. Co., 199 U.S.P.Q. 560 (T.T.A.B. 1978).

9. *In re* Clarke, 17 U.S.P.Q. 2d 1238 (T.T.A.B. 1990).

10. *See, e.g.*, U.S. Registration No. 5,040,974 (motion of rocket ship taking off for mortgage services).

11. *See, e.g.*, U.S. Registration No. 3,896,100 (leather texture of bottle for distilled spirits).

12. *See, e.g.*, Imagineering, Inc. v. Van Klassens, Inc., 53 F.3d 1260 (Fed. Cir. 1995) (appearance of furniture); Osem Food Indus. v. Sherwood Foods, Inc., 917 F.2d 161 (4th Cir. 1990) (product packaging).

qualify for protection.[13] In these scenarios, the marks in question generally are referred to as "trade dress," although the rules governing their protection are generally the same as those governing the protection of other marks.[14]

The Prerequisites for Mark Validity

To qualify for protection in the United States, a claimed mark must meet three requirements: (1) it must be used in commerce; (2) it must be distinctive, or, in other words, recognized by consumers as a mark; and (3) if it is nonverbal in nature, it must be nonfunctional. Each of these requirements is addressed below.

A Mark Must Be Used in Commerce

The Use in Commerce Requirement

Subject to the intent-to-use application process discussed below, trademark rights in the United States historically have been established through *use* of the mark in commerce:

> Rights can be acquired in a designation only when the designation has been actually used as a trademark . . . or when an applicable statutory provision recognizes a protectable interest in the designation prior to actual use. A designation is "used" as a trademark . . . when the designation is displayed or otherwise made known to prospective purchasers in the ordinary course of business in a manner that associates the designation with the goods, services, or business of the user. . . .[15]

---

13. *See, e.g.*, Two Pesos, Inc. v. Taco Cabana, Inc., 505 U.S. 763 (1992) (interior and exterior of restaurant); Original Appalachian Artworks, Inc. v. Toy Loft, Inc., 684 F.2d 821 (11th Cir. 1982) (sale of soft-sculpture dolls for adoption).

14. A significant exception is that, like colors, product configurations cannot be inherently distinctive. *See* TrafFix Devices, Inc. v. Mktg. Displays, Inc., 532 U.S. 23 (2001).

15. RESTATEMENT (THIRD) OF UNFAIR COMPETITION § 18, at 184 (1995).

This contrasts with the situation found in jurisdictions outside the United States, in which rights are created by registration.

How to Use a Mark

To demonstrate use in commerce under federal law, the claimant to a trademark must show that it has placed the mark on the goods (or on labels or tags affixed to the goods, packaging, or point of sale displays) and that the goods have been sold or transported in interstate commerce.[16] Likewise, to use a service mark, a claimant must use the mark on signage associated with its services or in advertising for the services and then provide the services in interstate commerce. The use in commerce standard is liberal but does not encompass token shipments or other dealings made merely for purposes of reserving a mark or obtaining or maintaining a registration.[17] In other words, the use must be "bona fide" commercial use, ideally in the form of a transaction with an unaffiliated end user of the goods or services provided under the mark.[18]

A trademark or service mark may be identified by placing the designation [TM] or [SM] adjacent to it. These designations are used to identify unregistered trademarks and indicate that trademark rights are claimed. Alternatively, an asterisk may be used instead of the [TM] or [SM] designation, with an explanation that the mark is owned by a particular entity.

The statutory ® notice indicates that a mark is federally registered in the USPTO.[19] Other forms of statutory notice include the words "Registered in U.S. Patent and Trademark Office" or "Reg. U.S. Pat. & Tm. Off."[20] Using the statutory notice constitutes constructive notice of registration and may preserve the right to collect damages for infringement of the mark without showing that the infringer had actual notice that the mark was registered.

---

16. Assuming a claimed mark otherwise meets the requirements for protection, it may qualify for protection under state law if it has not been used in interstate commerce.

17. *See, e.g.,* Scorpiniti v. Fox Television Studios, Inc., 918 F. Supp. 2d 866, 875 (N.D. Iowa 2013) (rejecting claim of priority of rights based on finding that plaintiff had made only token uses of its mark).

18. 15 U.S.C. § 1127; Lanham Act § 45.

19. 15 U.S.C. § 1111; Lanham Act § 29.

20. *Id.*

The ® symbol should not be used with marks that are not registered or in countries where the mark is not registered.

When a mark appears in print or other textual media, it should be distinguished from the surrounding text by use of a different type size or style (e.g., ALL UPPER CASE or *italics*) and the appropriate notice (®, TM, or SM). The trademark should be used in conjunction with a generic term for the goods or services to emphasize the "brand" aspect of the mark. The mark should never be used as a noun but instead only as an adjective modifying a noun. In fact, the word "brand" is often used with the mark to emphasize that the mark is a trademark, not the common name of a product. An example of this usage is "'Post-it'® brand notes" for adhesive-backed paper pads sold by the 3M Company.

A trademark owner must use its mark to maintain its rights. When use of a mark is discontinued with the intent not to resume use, the mark will be considered abandoned and unenforceable.[21] Failure to use a mark for three years is prima facie evidence that the mark has been abandoned.[22] In cases in which that evidence exists, the mark owner must produce evidence of its intent to resume use of the mark, ideally within the initial three-year period of nonuse.[23]

A Mark Must Be Distinctive

A mark must be distinctive, or recognizable as a mark, to serve its identification function. The degree of distinctiveness has important implications. Marks can be inherently distinctive, they can acquire distinctiveness with use, or they can lack distinctiveness altogether. Marks are typically classified as (1) arbitrary or fanciful, (2) suggestive, (3) descriptive, or (4) merely generic terms.[24] Generic terms can never be trademarks because they lack

---

21. *Id.* § 1127; Lanham Act § 45.
22. *Id.*
23. *See generally* Crash Dummy Movie, LLC v. Mattel, Inc., 601 F.3d 1387, 1391 (Fed. Cir. 2010).
24. *See* Abercrombie & Fitch Co. v. Hunting World, Inc., 537 F.2d 4, 9 (2d Cir. 1976).

distinctiveness;[25] descriptive terms are not inherently distinctive, but they can acquire distinctiveness with use; and suggestive, arbitrary, and fanciful terms are inherently distinctive and therefore protectable immediately upon the inception of their use.[26]

An arbitrary or fanciful mark bears no relationship to the associated goods or services. It therefore follows that such a mark is inherently distinctive and readily distinguishes one merchant's goods from those of another. A "fanciful" mark is typically composed of coined words, while an "arbitrary" mark uses words in common use but that bear no relationship to the associated goods. Fanciful marks include CLOROX, EBAY, GOOGLE, ROLEX, or PEPSI. Arbitrary marks include APPLE for computers, AMAZON for an electronic marketplace, VIRGIN for an airline, and GREY GOOSE for vodka.

A "suggestive" mark suggests some quality or character of the associated goods or services but not explicitly, so that some imagination is needed to determine the nature of those goods or services. Suggestive marks include JAGUAR for fast, luxurious cars, NETFLIX for an internet video streaming service, and EXPLORER for an internet search engine. Like arbitrary and fanciful marks, suggestive marks are inherently distinctive and readily registrable as marks.

In contrast, a "merely descriptive" mark identifies a characteristic, quality, purpose, or some other aspect of a good or service. A descriptive mark is not inherently distinctive and is protectable or registrable only if consumers have learned to associate it with a single source. This learned association is called "acquired distinctiveness" or "secondary meaning."[27] Marks found to be descriptive but that have acquired distinctiveness include CHAPSTICK

---

25. Although the phrase is widely used, "generic mark" is an oxymoron; a generic term is really not a mark at all.

26. *See* Two Pesos, Inc. v. Taco Cabana, Inc., 505 U.S. 763, 768 (1992) ("The latter three categories of marks, [suggestive, arbitrary and fanciful] because their intrinsic nature serves to identify a particular source of a product, are deemed inherently distinctive and are entitled to protection.").

27. *See generally* Zatarains, Inc. v. Oak Grove Smokehouse, Inc., 698 F.2d 786, 791 (5th Cir. 1983), *abrogated in part on other grounds by* KP Permanent Make-Up, Inc. v. Lasting Impression I, Inc., 543 U.S. 111 (2004).

for lip balm,[28] RAISIN-BRAN for breakfast cereal,[29] and VISION CEN-TER for a business offering optical goods and services.[30] At least in the registration process, the statute provides that a showing of exclusive and continuous use of the mark in commerce by the applicant for five years may be prima facie evidence of distinctiveness,[31] and some courts have adopted the same rule in context of infringement litigation.[32] Otherwise, the owner of a descriptive mark can demonstrate the acquired distinctiveness required for protection by submitting evidence of (1) the length and manner of its use, (2) the nature and extent of advertising featuring the mark, (3) the efforts made by the mark's owner to promote a connection in the public's mind between the mark and the owner, and (4) the extent to which the public actually identifies the name with the plaintiff's product or venture.[33]

A generic term is one used by the public to identify a category of goods, such as "beer," "shoes," or "automobiles," to which a particular product belongs, e.g., products sold under the MICHELOB, JORDAN, or PORSCHE CARERRA marks. A generic term can never be a trademark. Examples of terms found generic include "lite beer" for lower-calorie beer,[34] "shredded wheat" for cereal,[35] and "super glue" for a rapid-setting permanent adhesive.[36]

Nevertheless, a term that is generic for one product can be arbitrary when applied to another. For example, the word "trumpet" is generic for a type of musical instrument but would be arbitrary if used, for instance, in connection with laminate flooring. Furthermore, a term that is not initially generic may become so if consumers come to believe it is the name for a

---

28. *See* Morton Mfg. Corp. v. Delland Corp., 166 F.2d 191, 193 (C.C.P.A. 1948).

29. *See* Skinner Mfg. Co. v. Kellogg Sales Co., 143 F.2d 895, 898 (8th Cir. 1944).

30. *See* Vision Ctr. v. Opticks, Inc., 596 F.2d 111, 116 (5th Cir. 1979).

31. 15 U.S.C. § 1052(f); Lanham Act § 2(f).

32. *See, e.g.*, Stuart Hall Co. v. Ampad Corp., 51 F.3d 780, 789 (8th Cir. 1995).

33. *See, e.g.*, FN Herstal SA v. Clyde Armory Inc., 838 F.3d 1071, 1084 (11th Cir. 2016).

34. *See, e.g.*, Miller Brewing Co. v. G. Heileman Brewing Co., 561 F.2d 75, 81 (7th Cir. 1977).

35. *See, e.g.*, Kellogg Co. v. Nat'l Biscuit Co., 305 U.S. 111, 112-13 (1938).

36. *See, e.g.*, Loctite Corp. v. Nat'l Starch & Chem. Corp., 516 F. Supp. 190, 200 (S.D.N.Y. 1981).

type of product. Former marks that have become generic include "aspirin,"[37] "cellophane,"[38] "escalator,"[39] and "dry ice."[40]

A Mark Must Be Nonfunctional

A third prerequisite for trademark protection, or a "trade dress," which typically comes into play only if the claimed mark is nonverbal, is that the claimed mark is nonfunctional. There are two types of functionality that can disqualify a claimed mark for protection. The first is utilitarian functionality, which comes into play if the claimed mark is necessary to a product's utility or affects the product's cost and/or method of manufacture.[41] If it is found functional in the utilitarian sense, it is eligible only for patent protection. As the Supreme Court has observed, "[i]f a product's functional features could be used as trademarks . . . a monopoly over such features could be obtained without regard to whether they qualify as patents and could be extended forever (because trademarks may be renewed in perpetuity)."[42]

Although it can come into play in other contexts, the utilitarian nonfunctionality requirement often is the most difficult obstacle for parties seeking to protect product designs as marks. The fact that an underlying product serves a function—e.g., a chair provides support for sitting individuals—favors a finding the product itself is functional in the utilitarian sense. This does not, however, necessarily render its design ineligible for protection.[43] Rather, "[i]n trademark law, 'functional' means not that a feature serves a function; it means that the feature is one that competitors would find necessary to incorporate into their product in order to be able to

---

37. *See* Bayer Co. v. United Drug Co., 272 F. 505, 511 (S.D.N.Y. 1921).

38. *See* DuPont Cellophane Co. v. Waxed Prods. Co., 85 F.2d 75, 82 (2d Cir. 1936).

39. *See* Haughton Elevator Co. v. Seeberger, 85 U.S.P.Q. 80, 81 (Comm'r Pats. 1950).

40. *See* Dry Ice Corp. v. La. Dry Ice Corp., 54 F.2d 882, 884-85 (5th Cir. 1932).

41. *See* Inwood Lab'ys v. Ives Lab'ys 456 U.S. 844, 850 n.10 (1982).

42. Qualitex Co. v. Jacobson Prods. Co., 514 U.S. 159, 164-65 (1995).

43. "The design of a product may serve at least two purposes. It may identify the source of the product, and it can serve a utilitarian purpose." Fabrication Enters. v. Hygenic Corp., 64 F.3d 53, 55 (2d Cir. 1995).

compete effectively."[44] This inquiry requires addressing "whether the trade dress *as a whole* is functional," not whether individual features composing the dress are functional.[45]

To determine whether a claimed trade dress is necessary for effective competition and therefore ineligible for protection, courts typically look at a number of factors. The factor of perhaps greatest significance is the existence of a utility patent bearing on the design, as the Supreme Court has held the disclosure of a related utility patent is "strong evidence" of the utilitarian functionality of the underlying device.[46] Another factor historically playing a significant role in the utilitarian functionality analysis is the availability of commercially feasible alternative designs.[47] Courts weighing the utilitarian functionality or nonfunctionality of claimed marks also often consider whether a product's trade dress allows it to be manufactured more economically than competing alternatives[48] and whether the trademark claimant has touted the functionality of its design in promotional materials.[49]

The second type of functionality is aesthetic functionality. Although aesthetic functionality is more difficult to explain than utilitarian functionality, a claimed mark can be aesthetically functional if protection for it would put competitors of the claimed mark's owner at a significant non-reputation-related disadvantage.[50] Thus, for example, the color black has been found aesthetically functional for outboard motors[51] and when used on the packaging for floral arrangements,[52] because it made the motors appear smaller in the former context and because it connoted luxury in the latter context.

---

44. Vaughan Mfg. Co. v. Brikam Int'l, Inc., 814 F.2d 346, 349 (7th Cir. 1987).

45. Tools USA & Equip. Co. v. Champ Frame Straightening Equip., Inc., 87 F.3d 654, 658 (4th Cir. 1996).

46. *See* TrafFix Devices, Inc. v. Mktg. Displays, Inc., 532 U.S. 23, 29-30 (2001).

47. *See, e.g.*, Valu Eng'g, Inc. v. Rexnord Corp., 278 F.3d 1268, 1276 (Fed. Cir. 2002).

48. *See, e.g.*, Union Carbide Corp. v. Fred Meyer, Inc., 619 F. Supp. 1028, 1032 (D. Or. 1985), *aff'd sub nom.* First Brands Corp. v. Fred Meyer, Inc., 809 F.2d 1378 (9th Cir. 1987).

49. *See In re* Becton, Dickinson & Co., 675 F.3d 1368, 1375-76 (Fed. Cir. 2012).

50. *Id.* at 165.

51. *See* Brunswick Corp. v. Brit. Seagull Ltd., 35 F.3d 1527, 1533 (Fed. Cir. 1994).

52. *See In re* Florists' Transworld Delivery, Inc., 106 U.S.P.Q.2d 1784, 1787-92 (T.T.A.B. 2013).

Registration of Marks

The Benefits of Federal Registration

The law protects trademarks based on bona fide use in commerce subject to Congressional regulation.[53] Registration does not create enforceable trademark rights. Nonetheless, several very significant advantages are available to a mark owner registering its mark under federal law with the United States Patent and Trademark Office (USPTO).

If a mark is inherently distinctive (arbitrary, fanciful, or suggestive), or has become distinctive by having acquired secondary meaning, it can be registered on the USPTO's Principal Register. Immediately upon its issuance, a registration on the Principal Register is "prima facie evidence" of the validity of the mark, the registrant's exclusive right to use the registered mark, and the registrant's ownership of the mark,[54] which most courts hold shifts the burden of proof on those issues from the plaintiff to the defendant in any litigation to protect the mark.[55] An additional advantage to a registration on the Principal Register is that it constitutes nationwide constructive notice of the registrant's rights as of the filing date of the application from which it matured, meaning that a defendant adopting an infringing mark after that date cannot claim it did so without knowledge of the plaintiff's prior rights.[56] A registrant's rights may become "incontestable" after five years on the Principal Register, if an appropriate declaration is filed with

---

53. 15 U.S.C. § 1051; Lanham Act § 1.

54. 15 U.S.C. §§ 1057(b), 1115(a); Lanham Act §§ 7(b), 33(a).

55. *Compare* Checker Car Club of Am., Inc. v. Fay, 262 F. Supp. 3d 621, 626 (N.D. Ill. 2017) ("When the identifying word, term, name, symbol or device claimed as a trade name or mark is not registered with the United States Patent and Trademark Office, the burden is on the claimant . . . to establish that it is entitled to protection. . . .") *with* Ricks v. BMEzine. com, LLC, 727 F. Supp. 2d 936, 953 (D. Nev. 2010) ("If the mark has been properly registered, the burden shifts to the alleged infringer to show by a preponderance of the evidence that the mark is not protectable.").

56. 15 U.S.C. § 1072; Lanham Act § 22.

the USPTO.[57] Incontestability is "conclusive evidence" of validity and ownership of the mark and therefore can be an even more powerful offensive weapon in litigation to protect a registered mark.[58]

Marks do not receive these benefits if they are registered on the Supplemental Register, which is reserved for descriptive marks that have not acquired secondary meaning.[59] Nevertheless, registration of a mark on the Supplemental Register can provide actual (as opposed to constructive) notice to interested parties of the owner's claim to rights, may deter others from adopting and using the mark, will be cited by the USPTO as a basis for refusing to register confusingly similar marks, and provides a basis for registering the mark in many foreign countries. Moreover, registration on the Supplemental Register for five years may be used to prove exclusive use of the mark for that period, which is very helpful in proving distinctiveness for registration on the Principal Register.

How to Obtain a Federal Registration

For applicants domiciled in the United States, an application for registration must be based on either current use in commerce or a bona fide intent to use the mark in commerce.[60] If an applicant has not used the mark in com-

---

57. 15 U.S.C. § 1065; Lanham Act § 15. The requirements for a declaration of incontestability include that the registered mark has been used continuously for the five-year period immediately before the declaration's execution, that there has been no final judgment adverse to the registrant's rights to the mark, and that no challenge to those rights is pending. *Id.*

When a registrant has filed a declaration of incontestability, some courts and commentators refer to the registration itself as incontestable. *See, e.g.,* KP Permanent Make-Up, Inc. v. Lasting Impression I, Inc., 543 U.S. 111, 117 (2004).

58. 15 U.S.C. § 1115(b); Lanham Act § 33(b); *see generally* Park 'N Fly, Inc. v. Dollar Park & Fly, Inc., 469 U.S. 189 (1985).

59. 15 U.S.C. § 1094; Lanham Act § 26.

60. 15 U.S.C. § 1051; Lanham Act § 1. A third basis exists as well, which concerns filings based on foreign applications or registrations. That basis is available only to non-US entities with claims to the same mark in their home countries. Applicants using it must also aver a bona fide intent to use their marks in the United States. *See id.* § 1126(d)(2); Lanham Act § 44(d)(2). Although a non-US entity therefore can successfully register its mark without

merce but has a bona fide intent to do so, it can file an intent-to-use (ITU) application. An ITU application cannot mature into a registration until the applicant files a verified statement that it has used the mark in commerce. Nevertheless, and although priority of rights under US law ordinarily is determined by the dates on which parties to a dispute first used their respective marks, the procedural and substantive rights attaching to a registration will back date to the filing date of the underlying application, even if the application was filed on an intent-to-use basis.[61]

The USPTO examines trademark applications. An application is assigned to an Examining Attorney, who ensures that the application meets all statutory requirements and that the mark is registrable. Two of the most important determinations made by the Examining Attorney are whether the mark is distinctive as applied to the goods or services for which registration is sought and whether the mark is confusingly similar to a mark already registered or is the subject of an earlier-filed application.

If the Examining Attorney assigned to an application raises an objection to the applied-for mark's registration, the applicant will have three months in which to respond to the refusal, although an additional three-month extension can be purchased if necessary.[62] If the applicant cannot overcome any grounds for refusal asserted against an application, it can appeal the refusal to a tribunal of administrative law judges known as the Trademark Trial and Appeal Board ("TTAB"); if dissatisfied with the TTAB's disposition of its appeal, the applicant can then appeal either to the United States Court of Appeals for the Federal Circuit (if it is happy with the existing record) or a local federal district court (if it wishes to supplement the record).[63]

If the mark appears to be registrable, the USPTO will publish the application for opposition in the *Official Gazette*. During the 30-day period following publication, which can be extended for up to an additional 90 days without an applicant's consent, interested parties can oppose the registration of a mark. If no one successfully opposes an application, the USPTO will register the mark if the application is use-based, or it will issue a Notice of

---

use in commerce in the United States, it must so use the mark to enforce the rights to it. *See generally* Lodestar Anstalt v. Bacardi & Co., 31 F.4th 1228, 1248 (9th Cir. 2022).
61. 15 U.S.C. § 1057(c); Lanham Act § 7(c).
62. 37 C.F.R. § 2.62(a).
63. 15 U.S.C. § 1071; Lanham Act § 21.

Allowance for an ITU application. After the USPTO issues a Notice of Allowance, an applicant has six months, extendable in six-month increments for up to 30 additional months, to file a Statement of Use, together with specimens showing evidence of use. Assuming that all requirements are met by filing a proper Statement of Use, the USPTO will then issue a Certificate of Registration.

Registration provides protection for the use of the specific goods or services identified in the registration in connection with the mark as registered. When preparing advertising materials, promotional literature, or product labeling materials, it is important to compare these materials with the certificate of registration to make sure they depict the mark in the exact form as shown on the certificate. Although it is possible to amend a registration to reflect an updated presentation of a mark, that option is available only if the updated version creates the same commercial impression as the original.[64]

Maintenance and Cancellation of Federal Registrations

So long as the registrant complies with certain requirements and another party does not challenge it, a federal registration can conceivably be maintained forever. The primary requirement for maintaining a federal registration is the filing of a declaration of ongoing use (or excusable nonuse) between the fifth and sixth anniversary of the registration, between the ninth and tenth anniversary of the registration, and then every 10 years thereafter.[65] The registrant also must file a separate application for renewal of registration every 10 years.[66] As discussed above, a declaration of incontestability also may be filed once the registration has passed its fifth anniversary and if the underlying mark has remained in continuous use for the five years preceding the declaration's execution without an active challenge to the validity of the mark or registration at the time of that execution.[67]

---

64. 15 U.S.C. § 1057(e); Lanham Act § 7(e).
65. *See* 15 U.S.C. § 1058; Lanham Act § 8.
66. *See* 15 U.S.C. § 1059; Lanham Act § 9.
67. *See* 15 U.S.C. § 1065; Lanham Act § 15.

The fifth anniversary of a registration's issuance is significant for another reason. First, prior to that date, a registration may be canceled either by a court of competent jurisdiction or the TTAB for any reason that would have prevented its issuance in the first place,[68] including that the party challenging the registration enjoys the prior use of a confusingly similar mark.[69] Once a registration on the Principal Register is five years old, however, Section 14(3) of the Lanham Act dramatically limits the grounds upon which cancellation may be sought, eliminating in particular allegations that a mark is merely descriptive without secondary meaning or that the challenger to the registration was using its mark prior to the registrant.[70] This five-year statute of limitations is unavailable to owners of registrations on the Supplemental Register, however.

A federal registration also can be invalidated in one of two ex parte proceedings enacted through the passage of the Trademark Modernization Act, both of which became effective on December 27, 2021. The first, ex parte expungement,[71] allows challenges to registrations covering marks that have never been used in commerce for some or all of the goods or services listed in the registration. It primarily targets registrations issued to foreign entities and those based on foreign registrations rather than those based on

---

68. *See, e.g.,* Int'l Order of Job's Daughters v. Lindeburg & Co., 727 F.2d 1087, 1091 (Fed. Cir. 1984).

69. Not surprisingly, petitions for cancellation are frequent counterclaims in litigation involving federally registered marks. *See, e.g.*, Keebler Co. v. Rovira Biscuit Corp., 624 F.2d 366, 376 (1st Cir. 1980).

70. 15 U.S.C. § 1114(3); Lanham Act § 14(3); *see also* McDonnell Douglas Corp. v. Nat'l Data Corp., 228 U.S.P.Q. 45, 47 (T.T.A.B. 1985).

Significantly, the five-year statute of limitations on cancellation actions does not depend on the registrant's filing of a declaration of incontestability. *See, e.g.*, Imperial Tobacco Ltd. v. Philip Morris, Inc., 899 F.2d 1575, 1579 n.6 (Fed. Cir. 1990) ("[S]ection [14] is not dependent on the filing of a declaration under section 15 which provides incontestable rights of use . . . ."); W. Worldwide Enters. v. Qinqdao Brewery, 17 U.S.P.Q.2d 1137, 1139 (T.T.A.B. 1990) ("[A] registration that is over five years old may be cancelled solely on the grounds set forth in Section 14[3], irrespective of whether or not the owner of the registration has filed an affidavit under Section 15."). In other words, incontestability and the statute of limitations are separate and independent concepts that have only the fifth anniversary of a registration in common.

71. 15 U.S.C. § 1066a; Lanham Act § 16A.

use of the registered marks in commerce.[72] It is available to challengers only between the third and the tenth anniversaries of a registration's issuance.[73]

The second, ex parte reexamination,[74] permits challenges to use-based registrations, or, in other words, registrations whose owners averred under oath that their marks were used in commerce during the application process. Such may have been included in the initial application itself or, alternatively, as part of a statement of use or amendment to allege use. This mechanism allows the USPTO to reexamine the accuracy of the registrant's averment of use as of the filing date of that averment or the expiration of the deadline for such an averment, which the Trademark Modernization Act defines as the "relevant date."[75] It is not available once a targeted registration has passed its fifth anniversary.[76]

International Registration under the Madrid Protocol

Trademark rights are territorial in nature, meaning that, with the exception of some jurisdictions like the European Union, they begin and end at national borders. Consequently, there is no way to secure a single registration covering all countries in the world. A mark owner seeking protection in multiple countries should be prepared, therefore, to pursue individual registrations of its mark in those countries. One way it can do so is to retain local trademark counsel in each country of interest and have them file separate applications with those countries' national trademark offices.

An additional option, which often can be more cost-effective if a mark owner desires registrations in numerous countries, is to take advantage of a treaty known as the Madrid Protocol. Most industrialized countries, including the United States,[77] belong to the Protocol, which is administered by the International Bureau (IB) of the World Intellectual Property Organization

---

72. 15 U.S.C. §§ 1126, 1141f; Lanham Act §§ 44, 66.
73. 15 U.S.C. § 1066a(i)(1); Lanham Act § 16A(i)(1).
74. 15 U.S.C. §1066b; Lanham Act § 16B.
75. 15 U.S.C. § 1066b(b); Lanham Act § 16B(b).
76. 15 U.S.C. § 1066b(i); Lanham Act § 16B(i).
77. 15 U.S.C. §§ 1141–1141n; Lanham Act §§ 44–74.

(WIPO).[78] The Madrid system provides mark owners with a streamlined mechanism to register their marks in other member countries of the Protocol by filing a single application directly through the USPTO and then requesting extensions of protection to those countries.

A mark registered outside the United States through the Madrid Protocol must be based on one or more US applications or registrations. The Madrid system is equivalent to filing applications directly in foreign jurisdictions, and it often provides a more cost-efficient, streamlined manner for doing so than making individual filings in national trademark offices. Guidance for filing Madrid applications, including electronic forms for international applications, is available on the USPTO and WIPO websites.[79] Significantly, however, an application filed through the Madrid system in a particular country must meet that country's substantive requirements for registration. Consequently, although the IB may issue a document styled as an International Registration with extensions of protection to particular countries, the national trademark offices of one or more of those countries might still refuse registration to the mark covered by it. If that occurs, the mark owner may need to retain local counsel in those countries to address the refusal.

State Registration of Marks

Trademarks and service marks may be registered in every US state, the District of Columbia, and the Commonwealth of Puerto Rico. In general, state registration provides few of the advantages of federal registration. However, issuance of a state registration may constitute evidence of ownership and even the validity of the mark in that particular jurisdiction. Most important, entering the mark on a state register provides notice of

---

78. *See Madrid Agreement for the Repression of False or Deceptive Indications of Source on Goods*, WIPO, www.wipo.int/treaties/en/ip/madrid (last visited Oct. 5, 2020).

79. *Trademark Help – Madrid Protocol – International Application*, USPTO, https://www.uspto.gov/learning-and-resources/trademark-faqs#type-madrid-protocol (last visited Oct. 5, 2020); *How the Madrid System Works*, WIPO, https://www.wipo.int/madrid/en/how_madrid_works.html (last visited Oct. 5, 2020).

the owner's claim of rights to any parties who undertake a comprehensive trademark search.

Clearance Procedure

Before using a mark or applying to register it, a party should check for possible conflicts with marks currently registered, in use, or for which applications have been filed. The process for screening new marks generally involves conducting a free online search through the USPTO's records to locate directly conflicting federal registrations.[80] In the absence of such a direct conflict, online searches may be expanded to cover state registrations and certain directory and trade name sources. Many potential mark owners rely on commercial searching services, which maintain substantial databases and which employ search strategies that may be difficult or too costly to replicate using online services. If online screening for prior claims to similar marks in the USPTO and state trademark offices does not disqualify a mark, the next step is usually a commercial search that uses more sophisticated methodologies than those available elsewhere.

In most cases, the evaluation of a commercial search report requires a significant exercise of judgment based on experience and knowledge of case law. A typical commercial search report includes the following sections: (1) a federal section, containing existing, expired, canceled, abandoned, and pending claims of rights in the USPTO; (2) a state trademark registration section; (3) a common-law section, containing information on unregistered potential marks from a variety of published sources, including trade directories, new product publications, and advertising journals; (4) trade name databases; and (5) an Internet component. Although most courts hold that there is no affirmative duty to undertake clearance investigations,[81] the

---

80. The Patent and Trademark Office's website may be accessed at www.uspto.gov.

81. *See, e.g.*, Star Indus. v. Bacardi & Co., 412 F.3d 373, 388 (2d Cir. 2005) ("This Court has never held adoption of a mark with no knowledge of a prior similar mark to be in bad faith even in the total absence of a trademark search, much less on the basis of an allegedly flawed trademark search.").

potential consequences of failing to do so in the form of litigation expenses and the disruption of having to respond to a challenge can be significant.

Marks as Property

Assignments

A trademark or service mark symbolizes—and derives its value from—the goodwill associated with the mark and the business associated with the mark. As a property right, a mark exists only in connection with its associated product or service. A mark cannot validly be transferred apart from the goodwill it symbolizes, and a valid assignment therefore must contain an assignment of the goodwill associated with the mark.

To maintain rights in an acquired mark, the assigned mark therefore must be used on a product that is substantially similar to the product with which the trademark was used by the assignor. Accordingly, assignment of a mark may also require the transfer of any proprietary knowledge or equipment necessary to manufacture the product or offer the services sold under the mark. If steps are not taken to maintain some degree of continuity between the assignor's and the assignee's respective uses of the mark, the transfer of rights may be found to be an invalid assignment in gross, in which case the assignee's rights will date back only to its own use of the mark.[82]

Licensing

A mark owner may license rights under the mark, and, indeed, a properly drafted license can extend the mark owner's rights to goods and services it does not offer itself.[83] A valid licensing arrangement requires the licensor to maintain control over the nature and quality of the goods sold under

---

82. *See, e.g.*, Brown Bark II, L.P. v. Dixie Mills, LLC, 732 F. Supp. 2d 1353, 1358 (N.D. Ga. 2010).
83. 15 U.S.C. § 1055; Lanham Act § 5.

the mark. The quality assurance requirement protects the buying public by ensuring that consumers will receive the quality of goods or services that they associate with the mark. If a licensor fails to maintain the quality of the goods, the license is a "naked" one, and loss of trademark rights can result.[84] License provisions should at a minimum include acknowledgements of the licensor's right to control the nature and quality of the goods and its right to inspect the licensee's operation, the licensee's duty to provide samples of the goods bearing the mark upon the licensor's request, and the fact that use of the mark will inure to the licensor's and not the licensee's benefit.

Violations of Rights

Causes of Action for the Violation of Rights

United States law recognizes a number of mechanisms for protecting the rights of trademark and service mark owners. Those mechanisms include the following causes of action.

Infringement

In an infringement action under federal law, a plaintiff must prove by a preponderance of the evidence (more likely than not) that a defendant's use of the allegedly infringing mark will create a likelihood of confusion, mistake, or deception in the minds of the relevant public as to the source of goods bearing the infringing mark or as to sponsorship or approval of goods bearing the mark.[85] Confusion may arise through the use of a mark that is the same as, or similar to, an existing mark in connection with the same or similar goods or services. Although most states recognize certain other causes of action with different names, such as those for deceptive trade practices, liability under them also generally turns on the plaintiff's

---

84. *See, e.g.*, FreecycleSunnyvale v. Freecycle Network, 626 F.3d 509, 519 (9th Cir. 2010).
85. 15 U.S.C. §§ 1114(1), 1125(a)(1)(A); Lanham Act §§ 32(1), 43(a)(1)(A).

showing of likely confusion.[86] Finally, likelihood of confusion is the primary ground asserted in oppositions to pending applications for registration and challenges to existing registrations.[87]

In the most commonly applied test for measuring the likelihood of confusion between the parties' marks,[88] courts examine factors that include: the strength or notoriety of the plaintiff's mark; the degree of similarity between the plaintiff's and the defendant's mark; the degree to which the plaintiff's and defendant's goods or services are related; the likelihood of the plaintiff expanding its business into the same field of use as the defendant; the defendant's good faith in adopting its mark; evidence of actual confusion; the sophistication of the parties' customers; the cost of the products or services; and the quality of the defendant's goods or services.[89] In any given case, some factors will weigh more heavily than others. For example, proof of bad faith can be decisive because one who has set out to deceive may be presumed to have succeeded, no matter how inept the attempt;[90] it also can affect the availability of monetary relief. Likewise, some courts hold that

---

86. *See, e.g.*, Univ. of Ga. Athletic Ass'n v. Laite, 756 F.2d 1535, 1539 n.11 (11th Cir. 1985) (holding tests for liability under federal law and Georgia law to be identical).

87. 15 U.S.C. § 1052(d); Lanham Act § 2(d).

88. Other, less commonly invoked tests for infringement include whether there are material differences between diverted or altered goods resold by defendants and their authorized counterparts that have not been adequately disclosed, *e.g.*, *Societe des Produits Nestle, S.A. v. Casa Helvetia, Inc.*, 982 F.2d 633, 635 (1st Cir. 1992), whether once-genuine goods have been so materially altered that no disclosure can cure the resulting likely confusion, *e.g.*, *Cartier v. Aaron Faber, Inc.*, 396 F. Supp. 2d 356, 360 (S.D.N.Y. 2005), and the Second and Ninth Circuit's competing tests in cases in which the defendant has made a nominative fair use of the plaintiff's mark to refer to the plaintiff's own goods or services, *e.g.*, *International Information Systems Security Certification Consortium, Inc. v. Security University, LLC*, 823 F.3d 153, 156 (2d Cir. 2016), and *New Kids on the Block v. News Am. Publishing, Inc.*, 971 F.2d 302, 308 (9th Cir. 1992). If a defendant has incorporated an accused imitation of the plaintiff's mark into the title or content of a creative work, and assuming the defendant does not use the accused imitation as a mark for its own goods, the relevant test for infringement may be that found in *Rogers v. Grimaldi*, 875 F.2d 994 (2d Cir. 1989).

89. *See, e.g.*, Polaroid Corp. v. Polarad Elecs. Corp., 287 F.2d 492, 495 (2d Cir. 1961).

90. *See, e.g.*, Sun-Fun Prods., Inc. v. Suntan Rch. & Dev. Inc., 656 F.2d 186, 190 (5th Cir. Unit B 1981) ("[P]roof that a defendant chose a mark with the intent of copying [a] plaintiff's] mark, standing alone, may justify an inference of confusing similarity.").

"[t]here can be no more positive or substantial proof of the likelihood of confusion than proof of actual confusion."[91]

Counterfeiting

The Lanham Act distinguishes between a mark that is a "colorable imitation" of a registered mark and a "counterfeit" mark. A colorable imitation is a mark that "so resembles a registered mark as to be likely to cause confusion or mistake or to deceive."[92] In contrast, a counterfeit mark is a "spurious" mark that is "identical with, or substantially indistinguishable from, a registered mark."[93] Consequently, "counterfeiting is 'hard core' or 'first degree' trademark infringement and is the most blatant and egregious form of 'passing off.'"[94] Goods associated with a counterfeit mark are typically imitations of an article associated with a well-known registered mark. Those goods are usually priced significantly lower and are of lower quality than the genuine article.

Dilution

An action for actual or likely dilution generally can be brought only if the mark sought to be protected is famous, meaning it is widely recognized by the general consuming public of the United States as a designation of source of the goods or services of the mark's owner.[95] Fame is determined by evaluating all relevant factors, including the extent of actual recognition of the mark, the extent of sales of goods or services under the mark, the extent of advertising and publicity of the mark, and which party advertised/publicized the mark.[96] The owner of a famous mark may bring an action to stop another's use of a mark when the use is likely to cause dilution by

---

91. World Carpets, Inc. v. Dick Littrell's New World Carpets, 438 F.2d 482, 489 (5th Cir. 1971).
92. 15 U.S.C. § 1127; Lanham Act § 45.
93. 15 U.S.C. § 1116(d); Lanham Act § 34(d).
94. 4 J. Thomas McCarthy, McCarthy on Trademarks and Unfair Competition § 25.10 (5th ed).
95. 15 U.S.C. § 1125(c)(2)(A); Lanham Act § 43(c)(2)(A).
96. *Id.*

tarnishment or dilution by blurring.[97] Likely dilution can occur regardless of whether the parties compete with each other or whether the defendant's mark is or is not likely to cause confusion.[98]

Likely dilution by tarnishment occurs when an association arises from the similarity between the mark used and the famous mark that harms the reputation of the famous mark.[99] For example, the famous mark CANDYLAND for a children's game was diluted by tarnishment by the use of "candyland.com" for an Internet website containing sexually explicit material.[100] A finding of likely dilution by tarnishment also can occur if a defendant uses an imitation of a plaintiff's mark in connection with shoddy merchandise.[101]

Likely dilution by blurring occurs when a famous mark is used by someone other than the owner and that use impairs the mark's distinctiveness,[102] meaning its ability to identify and distinguish the owner's goods or services. For example, the use of the mark SAMSUNG for clothing, when it is already registered and known for telecommunications services, may cause the mark to become diluted by blurring. All relevant factors are considered when determining whether there is dilution by blurring, including the degree of similarity between the challenged mark and the famous mark, the famous mark's degree of inherent or acquired distinctiveness, the extent to which the owner of the famous mark is engaging in substantially exclusive use of the mark, the famous mark's degree of recognition, whether the user of the challenged mark intended to create an association with the famous mark, and any actual association between the challenged mark and the famous mark.[103]

At least at the federal level, a finding of liability for likely dilution cannot be based on a noncommercial use by a defendant.[104] That exclusion from

---

97. 15 U.S.C. § 1125(c)(1); Lanham Act § 43(c)(1). In contrast to the federal dilution statute, which requires a plaintiff to demonstrate likely dilution, some state dilution statutes require showings of actual dilution.

98. *Id.*

99. 15 U.S.C. § 1125(c)(2)(C); Lanham Act § 43(c)(2)(C).

100. *See* Hasbro, Inc. v. Internet Ent. Grp., 40 U.S.P.Q.2d 1479, 1480 (W.D. Wash. 1996).

101. *See, e.g.,* Gianni Versace, S.p.A., v. Versace 19.69 Abbigliamento Sportivo SRL, 328 F. Supp. 3d 1007, 1024 (N.D. Cal. 2018), *appeal dismissed,* No. 19-15188, 2019 WL 2005744 (9th Cir. Apr. 17, 2019).

102. 15 U.S.C. § 1125(c)(2)(B); Lanham Act § 43(c)(2)(B).

103. *Id.*

104. *Id.* § 1125(c)(3); Lanham Act § 43(c)(2)(C).

liability, however, is unavailable if the defendant uses its alleged imitation of the plaintiff's mark as a mark for its own goods or services.[105]

Cybersquatting

Enacted in 1999, the Anticybersquatting Consumer Protection Act (ACPA) prohibits the bad faith registration, trafficking in, or use of a domain name that is identical or confusingly similar to a distinctive mark, including a personal name, or that is likely to dilute a famous mark.[106] A mark owner may bring a civil action against the person liable; however, if a responsible defendant cannot be identified, a mark owner can bring an action against the domain name itself.[107]

To determine bad faith intent, a court generally considers factors such as whether the domain name registrant has made bona fide prior use of the name; attempted to sell the name to the mark owner without ever having used it; diverted consumers from the mark owner's online location; provided misleading false contact information when applying for registration of the domain name; or registered multiple domain names that are identical or confusingly similar to distinctive marks.[108]

The ACPA defines "traffic[king] in" as "transactions that include, but are not limited to, sales, purchases, loans, pledges, licenses, exchanges of currency, and any other transfer for consideration or receipt in exchange for consideration."[109] For example, Virtual Works registered the domain name vw.net unaware that VW was a common abbreviation for VOLKSWAGEN automobiles. Virtual Works demonstrated bad faith under the ACPA when it offered to sell the domain name to Volkswagen.[110] In a similar case, the owner of the domain name fordworld.com, who had no relation to the Ford Motor Company, trafficked in the domain name in violation of the ACPA when he registered the domain name and offered to sell it to Ford.[111]

---

105. *See* Jack Daniel's Props., Inc. v. VIP Prods. LLC, 599 U.S. 140, 159 (2023).

106. 15 U.S.C. § 1125(d)(1)(A); Lanham Act § 43(d)(1)(A).

107. 15 U.S.C. § 1125(d)(2)(A); Lanham Act § 43(d)(2)(A).

108. 15 U.S.C. § 1125(d)(1)(B)(i); Lanham Act § 43(d)(1)(B)(i).

109. 15 U.S.C. § 1125(d)(1)(E); Lanham Act § 43(d)(1)(E).

110. *See* Virtual Works, Inc. v. Volkswagen of Am., Inc., 238 F.3d 264, 270 (4th Cir. 2001).

111. *See* Ford Motor Co. v. Catalanotte, 342 F.3d 543, 549 (6th Cir. 2003).

Remedies available to the mark's owner usually are limited to "a court order for the forfeiture or cancellation of the domain name or the transfer of the domain name to the owner of the mark."[112] For example, Volkswagen received the right to use vw.net for itself because Virtual Works tried to profit in bad faith from Volkswagen's mark.[113]

Remedies for the Violation of Trademark Rights

Injunctive Relief

A prevailing plaintiff is ordinarily entitled to injunctive relief, provided it can make four showings, namely, that: (1) it has suffered an irreparable injury; (2) remedies such as monetary damages are inadequate to compensate for that injury; (3) considering the balance of hardships between the plaintiff and defendant, an injunction is warranted; and (4) the public interest would not be disserved by a permanent injunction.[114] Injunctive relief is far and away the most commonly ordered remedy in trademark cases. The precise terms of an injunction are subject to the court's discretion and can require, among other things, the immediate discontinuance of the infringing mark and, in rare cases, even the recall of goods bearing it,[115] the mark's discontinuance after a phase-out period,[116] or, alternatively, the defendant's use of a disclaimer of affiliation.[117] In cases arising from defendants' trafficking in

---

112. 15 U.S.C. § 1125(d)(1)(D)(i); Lanham Act § 43(d)(1)(D)(i).

113. *See Virtual Works*, 238 F.3d at 269–71.

114. *See generally* eBay Inc. v. MercExchange, LLC, 547 U.S. 388, 391 (2006).

Pursuant to Section 34(a) of the Lanham Act, 15 U.S.C. § 1116(a), a plaintiff able to demonstrate a violation of the Act enjoys a presumption of irreparable injury for purposes of the first of these factors. Nevertheless, that presumption can be rebutted. *See, e.g.*, Nichino Am., Inc. v. Valent U.S.A. LLC, 44 F.4th 180, 186-87 (3d Cir. 2022).

115. *See* Tecnimed SRL v. Kidz-Med, Inc., 763 F. Supp. 2d 395, 414-16 (S.D.N.Y. 2011).

116. *See, e.g.*, Pogrebnoy v. Russian Newspaper Distrib., Inc., 289 F. Supp. 3d 1061, 1073 (C.D. Cal. 2017) (three-month phase-out period), *aff'd*, 742 F. App'x 291 (9th Cir. 2018); Coryn Grp. II, LLC v. O.C. Seacrets, Inc., 868 F. Supp. 2d 468, 498-99 (D. Md. 2012) (eight-month phase-out period).

117. *See, e.g.*, Cottonwood Fin. Ltd. v. Cash Store Fin. Servs., Inc., 778 F. Supp. 2d 726, 761 (N.D. Tex. 2011).

goods bearing counterfeit imitations of federally registered marks, courts can even order the seizure of those goods.[118]

Interdiction of Imported Goods

Under the Customs Act, any articles imported into the United States bearing a counterfeit mark are subject to interdiction and forfeiture.[119] A mark owner seeking to avail itself of this remedy must register its mark with the USPTO and then record the registration with US Customs and Border Protection (which is a process separate from registration in the first instance). This remedy is most effective if the mark owner provides the agency with detailed information on incoming shipments of goods bearing counterfeit marks.

Monetary Relief

Legal actions to protect trademarks and service marks are rarely self-financing, meaning that neither party likely will be made whole for its investment into a case. Nevertheless, several categories of monetary relief are available to prevailing plaintiffs, and a prevailing defendant is potentially eligible to recover its attorneys' fees.

An Award of the Plaintiff's Actual Damages

A plaintiff demonstrating a violation of its trademark or service mark rights is eligible to recover its actual damages or, in other words, the out-of-pocket losses it suffered from the defendant's conduct.[120] Nevertheless, most courts require those losses to be linked to mistaken purchasing decisions by confused consumers.[121] Because of that rule, proving the amount of actual damages can be very difficult.

---

118. *See, e.g.,* World Wrestling Ent., Inc. v. Unidentified Parties, 770 F.3d 1143 (5th Cir. 2014).

119. 19 C.F.R. § 133.21(b). Forfeiture occurs in the absence of written consent of the trademark owner.

120. 15 U.S.C. § 1117(a); Lanham Act § 35(a).

121. *See, e.g.,* Grubbs v. Sheakley Grp., 807 F.3d 785, 802 (6th Cir. 2015) ("To recover actual damages, [the plaintiff] 'was required to establish that [the defendant's] Lanham Act violations proximately caused it to suffer monetary damages.'" (quoting Herman Miller, Inc. v. Palazzetti Imps. & Exps., Inc., 270 F.3d 298, 323 (6th Cir. 2001))).

Under the Lanham Act, monetary relief for infringement, including an award of actual damages, is ordinarily trebled in the absence of extenuating circumstances if a defendant intentionally counterfeits a registered mark. Moreover, under the Trademark Counterfeiting Act of 1984, a person intentionally trafficking in goods or services who knowingly uses a counterfeit mark in connection with those goods or services may be fined up to $2,000,000 and imprisoned for up to 10 years. An organization may be fined up to $5,000,000. For repeat offenders, the sanctions are even greater—up to $5,000,000 in fines and 20 years' imprisonment for an individual, and up to $15,000,000 for an entity.[122]

An Accounting of the Defendant's Profits

In addition to an award of its actual damages, a prevailing plaintiff can pursue the separate remedy of an accounting of the defendant's profits; most courts consider these remedies mutually exclusive, but there are relatively rare examples of judicial opinions entering both.[123] An accounting of profits is not automatic but instead lies within the discretion of the court, which may well determine that an injunction adequately vindicates the plaintiff's rights, especially if the defendant did not willfully violate those rights.[124] Nevertheless, willfulness is not a bright-line prerequisite for an accounting.[125]

If an accounting is ordered, the plaintiff need demonstrate only the defendant's sales.[126] At that point, most courts impose upon the defendant the burden of apportioning those sales between infringing and noninfringing sources.[127] The defendant then has the burden of proving deductible expenses from the resulting figure to yield its profits; if the defendant fails

---

122. 18 U.S.C. § 2320(a).

123. *See, e.g.,* Merriam-Webster, Inc. v. Random House, Inc., 815 F. Supp. 691, 701 (S.D.N.Y. 1993) ("Contrary to [the defendant's] assertions, the plaintiff's damage award under the Lanham Act may be cumulative: plaintiff may be awarded both defendant's profits and any damages sustained by the plaintiff."), *rev'd on other grounds*, 35 F.3d 65 (2d Cir. 1994).

124. *See, e.g.,* Fabick, Inc. v. JFTCO, Inc., 944 F.3d 649, 659 (7th Cir. 2019).

125. *See* Romag Fasteners, Inc. v. Fossil, Inc., 140 S. Ct. 1492, 1497 (2020).

126. 15 U.S.C. § 1117(a); Lanham Act § 35(a).

127. *See, e.g.,* WMS Gaming Inc. v. WPC Prods. Ltd., 542 F.3d 601, 608 (7th Cir. 2008).

to carry those burdens, it risks the court finding that the plaintiff is entitled to record the entirety of the defendant's sales as profits.[128]

Equitable Adjustments to Awards of Actual Damages and Accountings of Profits

The federal Lanham Act authorizes adjustments to an award of a plaintiff's actual damages or a defendant's profits. To begin with, section 35(a) provides that "[i]n assessing damages the court may enter judgment, according to the circumstances of the case, for any sum above the amount found as actual damages, not exceeding three times such amount";[129] the same provision also recites that "[i]f the court shall find that the amount of the recovery based on profits is either inadequate or excessive the court may in its discretion enter judgment for such sum as the court shall find to be just, according to the circumstances of the case."[130] Likewise, unless the court finds extenuating circumstances, section 35(b) essentially mandates the trebling of monetary relief if a defendant has been found liable for having intentionally trafficked in goods or services associated with counterfeit marks.[131]

Statutory Damages

The Lanham Act recognizes two scenarios in which a prevailing plaintiff can pass up an award of its actual damages and an accounting of the defendant's

---

128. *See, e.g.,* Entrepreneur Media, Inc. v. JMD Entm't Grp., 958 F. Supp. 2d 588, 597 (D. Md. 2013) (awarding entirety of defaulting defendants' estimated revenues); Purepecha Enters. v. El Matador Spices & Dry Chiles, 109 U.S.P.Q.2d 1944, 1948 (N.D. Ill. 2013) (same).

129. 15 U.S.C. § 1117(a); Lanham Act § 35(a); *see also* Merck Eprova AG v. BrookStone Pharms., LLC, 920 F. Supp. 2d 404, 431 (S.D.N.Y. 2013) ("Because the 'intangible benefits' that accrued to [the lead defendant] as a result of its Lanham Act violations are thus not fully reflected in a calculation of [the plaintiff's] damages, the Court will treble the lost profits damages award.").

130. 15 U.S.C. § 1117(a); Lanham Act § 35(a). Significantly, an adjustment under Section 35(a) can only be to compensate the plaintiff and not to penalize the defendant, which means that the Lanham Act does not authorize awards of punitive damages. *See generally* Skydive Ariz., Inc. v. Quattrocchi, 673 F.3d 1105, 1115 (9th Cir. 2012). Nevertheless, punitive damages may be available under state law, even if the Lanham Act does not provide for them. *See, e.g.,* Sunlight Saunas, Inc. v. Sundance Sauna, Inc., 442 F. Supp. 2d 1160, 1170 (D. Kan. 2006) (declining to disturb award of punitive damages under Kansas law).

131. 15 U.S.C. § 1117(b); Lanham Act § 35(b).

profits and instead choose to receive statutory damages. First, if the defendant has trafficked in goods bearing a counterfeit mark, the plaintiff potentially can recover between $1,000 and $200,000 per counterfeit mark per type of goods or services sold; if the defendant's conduct was willful, the upper limit of an award is increased to $2,000,000 per counterfeit mark per type of good.[132] Second, a defendant found liable for cybersquatting under the ACPA may have imposed upon it an award of statutory damages "in the amount of not less than $1,000 and not more than $100,000 per domain name."[133] The amount of an award of statutory damages is subject to the court's discretion and generally turns on the court's perception of the defendant's misconduct, but it also can be influenced by such considerations as the plaintiff's damages, the defendant's profits, whether the defendant cooperated in producing its records, and the need to deter future unlawful behavior by the defendant.[134]

Attorneys' Fees

Section 35(a) of the Lanham Act provides that the prevailing party in an ordinary case (whether the plaintiff or the defendant) can recover its reasonable attorneys' fees, but only if the case is an "exceptional" one.[135] Under this standard, a fee award may be warranted if the prevailing party stood out in terms of the strength of its litigating position or, alternatively, if the nonprevailing party litigated the case in an unreasonable manner.[136] In contrast, if a defendant's conduct rises to the level of counterfeiting, section 35(b) of the Lanham Act provides for an automatic award of the plaintiff's fees unless the court finds extenuating circumstances.[137]

---

132. 15 U.S.C. § 1117(c); Lanham Act § 35(c).

133. 15 U.S.C. § 1117(d); Lanham Act § 35(d).

134. *See, e.g.*, Coach, Inc. v. Horizon Trading USA Inc., 908 F. Supp. 2d 426, 437 (S.D.N.Y. 2012).

135. 15 U.S.C. § 1117(a); Lanham Act § 35(a).

136. *See, e.g.*, All. for Good Gov't v. Coal. for Better Gov't, 919 F.3d 291, 295 (5th Cir. 2019) (affirming award of fees to prevailing plaintiff based on the weakness of the defendant's case and the unreasonable nature of the defendant's litigation tactics).

137. 15 U.S.C. § 1117(b); Lanham Act § 35(b); *see also* Lorillard Tobacco Co. v. A & E Oil, Inc., 503 F.3d 588, 595 (7th Cir. 2007) (affirming finding that defendants had failed to demonstrate extenuating circumstances), *overruled in part on other grounds by* McCarter v. Ret. Plan for Dist. Managers of Am. Family Ins. Grp., 540 F.3d 649 (7th Cir. 2008).

About the Contributors

Theodore H. Davis Jr. is a partner in the Atlanta office of Kilpatrick Townsend & Stockton LLP, where he practices trademark and unfair competition law, including litigation before the Trademark Trial and Appeal Board and the Federal Circuit. He is a member of the American Bar Association's Board of Governors, a member of the American Intellectual Property Law Association's Board of Directors, and a former member of the Executive Committee of the International Trademark Association. A frequent author, speaker, and expert witness on trademark-related matters, he also has taught as an adjunct professor at the Emory University and the University of Georgia schools of law, as well as testified before Congress on trade dress and Internet issues.

Jay Erstling's career has combined intergovernmental service, law firm practice, and teaching. Jay was a senior official at the World Intellectual Property Organization (WIPO), where he served as Director of the Office of the PCT and played an influential role in the development of international intellectual property policy. He served as expert witness and consultant in intellectual property litigation in the US and abroad as Of Counsel at Patterson Thuente IP. And he continues to teach as an emeritus professor of international intellectual property law at Mitchell Hamline School of Law, the Vytautas Maagnus University Faculty of Law (in Lithuania), and the KDI School of Public Policy and Management (in Korea).

Megan Miller is an attorney at Winthrop and Weinstine, P.A. with extensive experience prosecuting trademark and patent applications as a paralegal before becoming an attorney, particularly under the Madrid and PCT systems. Megan's global technology practice comprises intellectual property (IP) prosecution and enforcement (including proceedings before the TTAB), data privacy compliance, IP due diligence in M&A

and other financing transactions, and drafting of technology agreements for compliance with multi-national laws. Megan also co-authored the 2023 ABA Intellectual Property Law Section publication *The Practitioner's Guide to the PCT,* 2nd ed. with her mentor and all-time favorite human, Jay Erstling.

About the ABA Section of Intellectual Property Law

From its strength within the American Bar Association, the ABA Section of Intellectual Property Law (ABA-IPL) advances the development and improvement of intellectual property laws and their fair and just administration. The Section furthers the goals of its members by sharing knowledge and balanced insight on the full spectrum of intellectual property law and practice, including patents, trademarks, copyright, design, and trade secrets. Providing a forum for rich perspectives and reasoned commentary, ABA-IPL serves as the ABA voice of intellectual property law within the profession, before policy makers, and with the public.

Title	Regular Price	ABA-IPL Member Price
ADR Advocacy, Strategies, and Practices for Intellectual Property and Technology Cases, 2nd Ed. (5370231)	$149.95	**$119.95**
ANDA Litigation, 3rd Ed. (5370243)	$379.00	**$295.95**
Antitrust Issues in Intellectual Property Law, 2nd Ed. (5370263)	$149.95	**$119.95**
Arbitrating Patent Disputes (5370229)	$89.95	**$74.95**
Careers in IP Law (5370204) (The ebook is complimentary with ABA-IPL Section membership)	$24.95	**$16.95**
Commercialization of IP Rights in China (5370241)	$119.95	**$95.95**
A Comprehensive Patent Practice Form Book (5370260)	$139.95	**$109.95**
Computer Games and Immersive Entertainment, 2nd Ed. (5370239)	$89.95	**$69.95**
Copyright Litigation Strategies (5370228)	$369.00	**$285.00**
Copyright Remedies (5370208)	$89.95	**$74.95**
Crash Course on U.S. Patent Law (5370221)	$39.95	**$34.95**
The DMCA Handbook, 2nd Ed. (5370234)	$79.95	**$64.95**
The Essential Case Law Guide to PTAB Trials (5370233)	$249.95	**$199.95**
The Essentials of Japanese Patent Prosecution (5370245)	$149.95	**$119.95**
Intellectual Property and Technology Due Diligence (5370236)	$219.95	**$179.95**
The Intellectual Property Law Handbook, 2nd Ed. (5620154)	$139.95	**$109.95**
IP Attorney's Handbook for Insurance Coverage in Intellectual Property Disputes, 2nd Ed. (5370210)	$139.95	**$129.95**
IP Protection in China (5370217)	$139.95	**$109.95**
IP Strategies for Medical Device Technologies (5370238)	$149.95	**$119.95**
IP Valuation for the Future (5370237)	$89.95	**$59.95**
The Law of Trade Secret Litigation Under the Uniform Trade Secrets Act, 2nd Ed. (5370242)	$369.95	**$295.95**
A Lawyer's Guide to Section 337 Investigations before the U.S. International Trade Commission, 4th Ed. (5370240)	$139.95	**$109.95**
Legal Guide to Video Game Development, 2nd Ed. (5370227)	$74.95	**$59.95**
A Legal Strategist's Guide to Trademark Trial and Appeal Board Practice, 4th Ed. (5370247)	$179.95	**$144.95**
New Practitioner's Guide to Intellectual Property (5370198)	$89.95	**$69.95**
Patent Claim Drafting Practice (5370259)	$179.95	**$144.95**
Patent Freedom to Operate Searches, Opinions, Techniques, and Studies (5370230)	$139.95	**$109.95**

Title	Regular Price	ABA-IPL Member Price
Patent Trial Advocacy Casebook, 3rd Ed. (5370124)	$149.95	$119.95
Patently Persuasive (5370206)	$129.95	$99.95
The Practitioner's Guide to the PCT, 2nd Ed. (5370261)	$139.95	$109.95
The Practitioner's Guide to Trials Before the Patent Trial and Appeal Board, 3rd Ed. (5370258)	$169.95	$139.95
Pre-ANDA Litigation, 3rd Ed. (5370256)	$349.00	$259.00
Preliminary Relief in Patent Infringement Disputes (5370194)	$119.95	$94.95
Right of Publicity (5370215)	$89.95	$74.95
Settlement of Patent Litigation and Disputes (5370192)	$179.95	$144.95
Starting an IP Law Practice (5370202)	$54.95	$34.95
Summary of Covenants Not to Compete (5370244)	$179.95	$144.95
The Tech Contracts Handbook, 3rd Ed. (5370248)	$42.95	$33.95
Trademark and Deceptive Advertising Surveys, 2nd Ed. (5370255)	$189.95	$151.95
What Is a Copyright, 4th Ed. (5370257)	$19.95	$16.95
What Is a Patent, 4th Ed. (5370262)	$19.95	$16.95
What Is a Trademark, 5th Ed. (5370254)	$19.95	$16.95

Find these and other ABA-IPL books at ShopABA.com

Thank you for your order!

Jeff Salyards
Executive Editor, ABA Publishing
jeff.salyards@americanbar.org

Tax, shipping and handling charges may apply.
See web store for complete details and current shipping and handling rates and information.